VIOLET SEA GREEN DUSK FALCON

The poems in this extraordinary collection shimmer with light and color, vibrate in the imagination with almost hallucinatory effect. They reach the reader, through the intimate short-cuts of the senses, so powerfully that the gorgeous, daring language feels inevitable—just right—even as it leaves objective order behind.

But of all the many things that Mary Meriam does just right, the one that moves me with almost painful force is the way she conveys the effect of the absence of a loved one. She knows how to render, in physical terms, the fear of time, the appallingly blank view of the future that reduces bereaved or abandoned people—widows, for example—to the status of objects, as in this sestet from a sonnet titled "No More":

> *Because sun shines, and sleep has done with me,*
> *I rise, and brush my hair, and dress me—then*
> *I wonder what I am, and how to be,*
> *and who has made me so. It's time again*
> *to wash the dishes—then it's afternoons—*
> *then evenings come, with waxing, waning moons.*

Poem after poem in a rich variety of expertly handled forms—"The Mockers," "Ars Poetica," "Dusk," for instance—reveals the nature of love: its capacity to sow guilt, regret, longing, obsessive memory, fantasy; its tendency to inhabit every thought, experience, and sensation, and not only with our permission, but at our insistence. The speaker of "Dusk" says:

> *I'll run and dive into the shadow light*
> *to swim the coolly emerald silky lake*
> *or else to drown, to do what it will take*
> *to reach you in the silver sea tonight.*

Amazing, this cry of universal need, despite the perceived strangeness of love in unfamiliar guises still considered, by some, as unorthodox, even deep into the twenty-first century. More amazing still is the way this book succeeds in humanizing that cry and rendering it recognizably ours, at long last. It's about time.

—**Rhina P. Espaillat** author of *And After All* and *Agua de dos ríos/ Water from Two Rivers*

In ambitious and dextrous poems employing a variety of formal guises, Mary Meriam creates for us an impressionistic yet incisive vision of love and loss in her powerful new collection, *My Girl's Green Jacket*. Recalling the sonnets of John Donne and the religious ballads of Christina Rossetti, Meriam's assured poems pulse with a channeled intensity, leading us as readers through an emotional and intellectual landscape where we appreciate Eve and the apple in a new light, reconsider the aftermath of the flood, and see the author transformed into a renaissance queen: "You will remember me, the queer-voiced Mary, / gripping her falcon." A collection as brilliant as it is emotionally nuanced, *My Girl's Green Jacket* offers us a complex imaginative mirror to hold up against our current reality.
—**Stu Watson** editor of *Prelude*

Mary Meriam's *My Girl's Green Jacket* is rich in description, rhymes and rhythms, bedecked in vivid color and emotions undimmed by the veneer of irony that shellacs so many contemporary poems. Like the moon she describes in "It Gets Very Dark until the Moon Rises," Meriam's songs, stories, prayers, fairy tales, ghazals and love-cries shine, grow, and give the dark a dream.
—**Joy Ladin** author of *Fireworks in the Graveyard*

This stunning collection of verse by Mary Meriam presents a palette of poems in various hues and forms—sonnets, sestinas, ghazals. Silver, gold, jade green, and violet, a spectrum of color reflects this poet's sense of loss and longing through a synesthesia that helps us hear, taste, and feel pigmentation as thought and emotion. Openly, avowedly lesbian, these poems are frankly romantic, lyrically linking her beloved to land, lake, and sky. Meriam notices the world quietly, yet vibrantly, alive to its potency, and we savor it too, dazzled by the poet's keen, discerning eye.
—**Janice Gould** author of *The Force of Gratitude*

Lush, acrobatic, heartbroken, and witty by turns, or all at once, Mary Meriam's poems pack plot, memory, landscape, and longing into firm and elegant shapes. To call this work formally accomplished isn't sufficient. Meriam's lyricism is nervous and incandescent; her poems coruscate and spin. *My Girl's Green Jacket* honors not only the urgency of desire but also its mercurial restlessness. Poetic forebears ranging from Sappho to Hopkins, from H.D. to Marilyn Hacker, turn out to be not only generative models but also anchors in a world of relentless change.
—**Rachel Hadas** author of *Poems for Camilla*

Awe is equal parts nightmare and pleasure. Awe, in the hands of a poet, is exquisitely and horrifyingly impassioned. Mary Meriam's *My Girl's Green Jacket* writes the labor of our awe. Meriam stealthily interrogates our humanity by way of near-perfect poetic form, taking us through the nightmare that is "[t]he hell it is, a hell I said, / a monster swamped in plastic bags" and marching us all the way back to ourselves. But do not fret. Meriam leaves us with love. Meriam writes: "Nothing normal has ever happened to me." I say: Thank God.
—**kathryn l. pringle** author of *obscenity for the advancement of poetry*

Books by Mary Meriam

Full-Length Collections
Girlie Calendar
Conjuring My Leafy Muse

Chapbooks
The Lesbian
Word Hot
The Poet's Zodiac
The Countess of Flatbroke

Anthologies
The Lillian Trilogy
Lavender Review
Lady of the Moon
Irresistible Sonnets

Children's Book
Nuts in Nutland

My Girl's Green Jacket

My Girl's Green Jacket

Mary Meriam

HEADMISTRESS PRESS

Copyright © 2018 by Mary Meriam
All rights reserved.

ISBN-13: 978-0998761084
ISBN-10: 0998761087

This book may not be reproduced, in whole or in part, including illustrations, in any form (beyond that permitted by Sections 107 and 108 of the U.S. Copyright Law and except by reviewers for the public press), without written permission from the publishers.

Cover art by Florine Stettheimer. Costume design ("Georgette") for artist's ballet *Orphée of the Quat-z-arts*. Ca. 1912. Gouache and lace on paper on wood, 18 x 12 7/8" (45.7 x 32.7 cm). Gift of Miss Ettie Stettheimer. Digital Image © The Museum of Modern Art/Licensed by SCALA / Art Resource, NY

Cover & book design by Mary Meriam.

PUBLISHER
Headmistress Press
60 Shipview Lane
Sequim, WA 98382
Telephone: 917-428-8312
Email: headmistresspress@gmail.com
Website: headmistresspress.blogspot.com

for Lillian

Contents

SEDUCTIVE VIOLET SOFA

The Violet Stars of Dream's Day	1
From the Notebooks of Margaret Mead	2
Life Study	3
Alone in Love	4
Sentimentality	5
A Political Poem with Emotional Parts	11
Silver Necklace	15
It Gets Better	17
She Rose	18
Sapphic Palette	20

GHETTO ON THE FRAUGHT SEA

The Golden Box	23
Dance of the Violent Calendar	24
Attack of the Fanatics	25
States	26
Map	33
The Natural World	34
I would stand here forever for you	35
Borderline	37
[I cried a river then crossed the river]	39

WADING DEEPER IN GREEN WAVES

The Earth	43
The Sad Palace of Ill Effects	44
Godless	45
Liebegott	46
Pepper Mill	47
Mother Farewell	48
Psalm of the Sweetest Water	49
Culture en Femme	51
In the Healing	52
Deus ex Machina	53
Odd Girls	56

A MOVING JEWEL AT DUSK

Dusk	65
It Gets Very Dark until the Moon Rises	66
No More	67
Across the Lake	68
Return Address	69
Airstrikes in April	70
Ars Poetica	71
Mother Nature	72

GRIPPING HER FALCON

In the Sierra Nevadas	75
Herself	76
Spring in the Mountains	77
Crows	79
The Sky	80
The Mockers	81
Sapphics	82
Notes on a Lost Quote	83
Gender	84

Notes	87
Acknowledgments	89

SEDUCTIVE VIOLET SOFA

The Violet Stars of Dream's Day

One day my dream runs that way down the road,
road-runner rustling past the country yards
without a getup, backup, rusty, slowed
by practice in her ragged leotards,
a dream that isn't blessed with flesh or power,
cranky, no credit, artsy, quick, and dying
from being locked inside a monster's tower
for fleeing on her bicycle and flying.
Her language isn't yours. You may not speak to her.
Gingerly slide your body sideways in her bed,
and calm her psoas muscle, stroke her kitten fur,
and keep your eyelids closed against your heavy head.
If you are good and brave, my dream will sew a blue
elaborate gown with violet stars to rain on you.

From the Notebooks of Margaret Mead

I have been invited to
your parties and weddings
your birthdays and holidays
though I do not attend

your parties and weddings
your travels and meetings
though I do not attend
I become like you

your travels and meetings
my source of seeing
I become like you
in the sense of walking alone

my source of seeing
as one might imagine sea spray
in the sense of walking alone
through the mind at night

as one might imagine sea spray
and the warm light of day
through the mind at night
the comfort of bed

and the warm light of day
make a party of my longing
the comfort of bed
a wedding of my wishes

make a party of my longing
your birthdays and holidays
a wedding of my wishes
I have been invited to

Life Study

Sometimes I could cry about
the amount of work I do in one day.
Let me not list, let me not repeat.
But come inside to my longing dreams
where hard work turns to soft love
and her hands hold my hips
that call for touch like loons on the lake
that shimmers cool jade and hot gold at sunset.
Let me think about her lips
as sweet as strawberries
I bought from the one-armed farmer
with the psychedelic shirt who probably
fought in Vietnam by the ghosts on his face.
See how thoughts of her paint my mind with art
though I imagine art comes to life sometimes.

Alone in Love

She isn't mine. I am alone in love.
Inside my mind and soul, I moan in love.

The sound is pearly shell. The sound is slight,
only a cell of sound, a stone in love.

My flower bed so lavishly in bloom,
my elm tree's swelling leaves, my own in love.

Those fragile fantasies of love I drew
erased in anguish, overthrown in love.

She hasn't ears and eyes for this, old fool.
Impossible, your monotone in love.

Just face it, Mary, time is running short.
Love less, or you will die alone in love.

Sentimentality

Perfume

The scent of unknown flowers in the breeze
filling my curtains, makes my heart beat fast,
faster and faster. Would you answer, please,
would you answer this soul, this flesh at last?
So spring breaks me with thunderstorms of leaves
and fields of dainty flowers, stems that have
the hardest work to do with empty sleeves,
nothing to give, no one to hold and love,
nothing but dreams and sighs and broken trees
that stand alone in wilderness and fear
still unaddressed and bare, as if the freeze
of letters never left, would never veer
to warmth, the solitude of light and birds,
mock orange stifled in me with my words.

Roses

She doesn't make a fuss or say goodbye.
She gives me dates: departure and return.
She waits until she's just about to fly
to let me know, and I am left to burn
a thousand wonderings that wander through
my sweet-scorched mind like petals of red flowers.
This thought, this thought, this thought, of hopeful hue
(but most, despair) pursue me through the hours
as if their scent were mine and I could drink
her deeply, freely, closely, slowly, she
of me, and me of she. The rose is pink
in June and sends perfume delightfully
to those who buzz close by. But those who wait
keep watching through the hard departure gate.

Kitten

I sit with crow calls in the full-leafed trees
and other singing sounds, a symphony
of screech, hoot, trill, and melody
conveying messages of me me please.
Beyond the screen, trios of sipping bees.
Inside the screen, I call to Emily
who sleeps in humid air, tucked tidily
in her own cardboard box, a cat at ease.
This morning by the lake with maple leaves
green as July and fat with rain, my cat,
a recent rescue, scrawny, scared, and shy,
tells me how terrible it was, and that
she loves the fish I give her, and she'll try
to trust me soon, her sweet recitatives.

Seagulls

Here in the darkening of day, my dear,
I wear the hot pink top and leaves turn gold,
and you and I, apart, keep growing old.
I wonder if we nonetheless cohere,
or if my heart twigs dream a different tree.
Is lonesomeness my river's branch of woe?
How can I know, how can we ever know,
without the simple touch of salty sea.
Open or closed, the valves and locks of love
carry my vessel past the scent of pine.
I'm pulsing somewhere faster down the line.
You wave while seagulls scavenge from above
for morsels to sustain them, just as I,
a pile of leaves on fire, scorch the sky.

Wine

What could October ever satisfy
drinking the dregs of summer's last heatwave,
waking in sweaty sheets—no, that's a lie.
My sheets were cool and perfect as a cave
more underground than hell, an icy den
where winter waits to kill. It isn't far
to loss, until I go to bed again,
as distant as a worm is from a star.
I find no one is waiting for me there,
and what have I to say besides to her?
To her who holds for me a bed and chair
making of outer space a loving stir.
I'd leave the earth and every place I know—
would I? No god can tell me not to go.

Postcard

I watch the changing painting on the lake
at 3 o'clock in late November. Find
me here. Look harder. See I am an ache
on Owl Creek Cove and in my house confined,
a shadow on the glass I stand behind.
Outside, the painting changes while inside
only a dream. The sycamores aligned
along the shore become lit lines astride
still water. The waves and wind have died
so loveliness in gray, deep green, bright white
mirrors the land and sky. May I abide
my mind at dusk, a flock of doves in flight
while dark descends and colors disappear.
Let me go from here and hold her near.

Party

The green lake grays at dusk and grows more bleak
in January winter, sleety rain
stinging the waves. Another end of week
and end of day. And then a sweet slow stain
of silver spreads across the lake, some light
not quite extinguished glistens secretly,
maybe the code to open doors at night
to underwater rooms with company.
I sway there, sinking fast, you look away.
The oaks and maples, black and slick and bare,
quiver and lean, unsteady. It won't stay
the silver light of dusk, a light too rare
for dark. Before it disappears, I go
beneath the cold veneer to see and know.

Sister

She's in the sky, the trees, the rain, the ground,
she's safe or sick or dead for all I know.
One missing sister, not in sight, no sound
or touch, no fingertip or tip of toe.
How could she leave me so, how could she go
and dump me in this solitary heap.
I have one sister love, my sister crow,
my only fair and favorite one to keep.
But how can I complain of losing her
when loss is all my sister ever had.
Arrives the lovely sky of evening blues,
the sleeping trees their peaceful budding blur,
the angry rain is done, the world is mad,
the yellow daffodils break through the bruise.

Moonlight

Alert for cosmos, I forget myself
and scrape my toe against a door too swift.
Eclipse is soon. Is that a breeze I felt
or is the mighty Sun's blue sky less lit?
I've watched so many evenings sink to night.
Now noon, are shadows gathering? I wait
for any sign of disappearing light.
The forest buzzes, hums. I contemplate.
Is this an evening lack of breeze? The lake
lies flat and still. O Moon! You take a path
outside my latitude. I feel an ache
for total darkness; send your lunar breath.
Here is a hush and dimness, Mary child,
the Earth is still, half-lit and half-beguiled.

Kiss

I can't bear growing old like this, my hand
won't write the thought, my eyes won't see the print.
I only want to sing and play and dance,
be limber-fresh. It ended in a blink.
And now I gnaw my mouth that wants to kiss,
fight off the creeping agonies of flesh,
the sharp knife-jab of nerves (remember bliss?),
the twisted shots of bone and muscle stress.
Grow up, I scold myself as one more loss
batters my heart. You have your life and health.
You walk, you eat, you sleep. You almost lost
the greatest treasure, witch, your steady breath.
Stop sucking sour grapes and see this view:
the richly colored fall leaves fall, like you.

Spring

Without you, loss would wear a winter face.
What would I do? I couldn't wait for spring.
My oak tree's leaves are wrinkled, dry, defaced.
What would a change to warmer weather bring?
I'd feel the loss the same in every season,
just as I feel it now, alone out here,
November gray, with downed leaves wildly fleeing.
I'm serious, don't leave me in the air.
The lake waves ride the wind, can't let you go.
There's one last maple's golden gown still on.
The love I crave is cool and kind and slow
and how will I go on if she is gone
with never having breathed the air she breathes?
So chill me, wind, again, so I can grieve.

A Political Poem with Emotional Parts

1
When is the last ferry leaving for the island
Take me there now I need to get away
I need to see again how to live naked and shy

You wait for me there I can almost see you
Swaying in the hammock with important papers
Where is my cool drink where is my palm tree

I would like to see your large white hat in the breeze
Swaying in the hammock with important papers
Steady and salty the ocean rocks us to sleep

Where the glass frost melts and shivering ceases
A warm glance hot sand juicy citrus fruits
The past and the future snowballing in bed

2
It visits me with tantalizing tone
making a rainbow of my tears and sighs
then leaving, disconnects the telephone.
I'm dreaming backwards through our history
to hold the sound inside with silken ties
and piece together notes with memory.
How could she leave me
                          like this
lonely
                                      now?
Except there isn't anywhere to go
in air, in air I breathe, in everything
she might have said.

3
I love the way you love with all your heart
so that I feel it half a world apart.
A world, and then another world, until
the multiplying spaces crash my sill
and blow the curtains down
                                   a fragmentary
intrusion, like the weight of being merry
the night my reason dies
                            I'd like to reach
another shore and walk along the beach
if only all the waves weren't crashing down
dragging me deeper under. Another town,
another place to put my bed and table,
for you to love me more. But I'm unable.

4
I wonder
If life is only winter
Spring only
A dream

If life is only winter
How can I thrum
A dream
Into lily and leaf

5
Stress may trounce you, trouble pursue you, weakness
trick you, true. But darling I stand here waiting,
failings fleeing, feelings inflowing, flowers
thriving in dozens,

hundreds, millions. Kisses of snowdrops crop up,
baby polkadots in dull-flooded meadows
sensing yes again as the sunlight mythos
frees you from winter.

6
I confess
I want to be with you in every possible way
You have filled my mind with wild apple trees

You have often wandered through my meadows
You have released the mourning doves to the sky
You have picked a wild red apple

7
Daisy days of June, my pale-purple flower
Fill the fields with grasses and green excitement
See the sunlight, serious beams of sunlight
Sycamores tower

Yellow-petaled Susans grow wilder and wilder
Close your eyes, come closer and closer, kiss me
Daisy days of June, my pale-purple flower
Rain storms are over

8
How they carpet the marshy part of a yard
Lit from inside like a green planet
Sprung from the cold cold winter ground

When the spring rain runs dry on Monday
I'll go look at the blue violets blooming open
Under the hot new spring sun

Would you put your boots on in my house
And walk in the yard with me one day
See the lake and the great blue herons

But mostly the wild blue violets in the spring
The fresh earthy scent of them around us

9
I see you in person
a flame, and I become a flame
a flower, and I become a flower

your voice arriving inside me
like a memory or a dream
I become your flowing sentences

your breath in my ear a soft pulsing
your dear eyes attentive to me
your ankles navy

your breast crimson
close to the inviolate autumn sky
you are the golden afternoon

10
And yellow-brown leaves fallen on the ground
The mellow air breathable and here we go
Lesbian lesbian lesbian lesbian lesbian

A milieu of watery eyes and clouds
An island word an ancient word a lovely word
A condition without a home in high culture

You may prefer another word or hate lesbian
I prefer to make a bold simple statement
You may feel shadowed by the unserious

You may wish to be quiet and invisible
My female parts love her female parts
This is a political poem with emotional parts

Silver Necklace

The poet is in her early twenties and unable to face the deep, terrible problem of her life, the question of why she is alive, and how she will go on living. She hardly knows where she is, some different part of the country, in solitude, as always. The truth is that the losses and traumas of her life thus far have made her suicidal. She doesn't want to die, but she has only questions, no answers. Fire is red, and the rain makes red even deeper. Fire and water are conflated, burning, flooding, dying. May she keep her heavy head safe and hold on.

The poet is invisible. As if anyone were ever with her, as if she hadn't already lost everyone. She's remembering her recent trip with Sophie to a tropical island. Sophie gave her a silver necklace (long since lost). Like God, or a prince, or a priest, bringing her a silver necklace, Sophie visits her in this place where she sleeps, held in a half-alive stupor, being acted upon, unable to act, drifting through rooms and visions, unable to even imagine intimacy. Again, there's alarm about finances. But she can't wake up to it, she's too helpless and swamped with sadness and mystery. Even as she writes these lines, she can't quite believe she is writing them.

The poet as gardener at Sophie's beautiful old house in White Creek, with the creek and the bridge. It's good to see her awake and full of purpose. If she could only be guided this way into a steady life. How hopeful she is that the disaster can be repaired and forgotten, that fresh new grass will cover the mud. We see that no matter how hopeless she feels, there are always colors. Sophie, an artist, is inspiring her. Red, silver, emerald, yellow, darkness and light, the colors and the settings have beauty, but the sad truth is that another flood can be imagined, or else why mention it? Perhaps we'll never get used to the bridge's evenness or ever forget the downward tilt into flood. After all, landscaping is superficial, and an October afternoon's effort won't actually rescue anyone.

The poet in the tropics with Sophie, overwhelmed by colors, attempts art. But the vacation seems surreal and decadent to her. She's too worried by troubles, the landscape being eaten, the pretty yachts remote. If she could only surrender to the beauty. The language is too strange. She's never at home except in cold trouble. She doesn't fit in the natural order of the world. Is it because she loves Sophie? Or is it that her heart was beaten into a bloody pulp by old tragedies, and loving anyone or anything again is impossible. She tries to speak, to study, to draw, but still feels imprisoned in her disability. This is what happens when one runs from truth too difficult to swallow. But how can she face it alone, how can she even make sense of it?

The poet is at Sophie's house for a visit. They are no longer lovers. The poet is about to be obliterated by thirst. Boiling water sounds like art. She has no home, only the shut sky of a city mind. She's so hungry, she hallucinates a painting into life. If she could only hallucinate herself into life, make her dried self unfold and flower. Could she possibly be more alone as she climbs the hill behind Sophie's house and looks down at the cars passing, her only company? How to catch on fire, how to find home, how to breathe, and how to be less broken, and why, and for whom. She's still young, not even thirty, yet look at her disbelief and blackness, her failed crop and burs.

It Gets Better

You didn't tell me it was all about the red
ball of the sun, the sucking sky, the doubting orange.

Why am I camping in these woods? O flaming yellow
am I, a fire in my dress of girl-scout green.

The party wild, the artists high, the music blue,
you turn to me, a stranger out of indigo.

You take me to your studio's seductive violet
sofa, make love to me until I shout in violet.

So how could I have known I'd lose the indigo
last night? Kiss me now without a doubt in blue.

We live together in a house of sheaves of green,
sweet-scented flower fields around us sprouting yellow.

Fridays I bring you marigolds and peel your orange.
Hurry, my horse's racing heart is stout and red.

She Rose

Born dancing like a bloody fool
in utero in tap-dance school,
she's a baby you can see
will reap a heap of tragedy.
Dip and twitch, around she goes
and throws her audience a rose

it fails to catch; my poor, poor Rose
auditions for the part of fool.
She knows exactly how it goes.
She shames the elementary school.
But this is not a tragedy.
Pass me a tissue. Let me see.

Born sailing on a squally sea,
her savage shadow sailed and rose
to heights of such dumb tragedy
that now she plays the peasant-fool
in *Taming of the Shrew* in school.
Stand up and balance. Down she goes.

Release and rise. And down she goes.
She plays the troll who cannot see
the trouble she's in after school.
Pledge allegiance to the rose
for whom it stands, a mighty fool
adept at making tragedy

not quite a total tragedy.
Her shadow dances where it goes.
Look, her red-bud is no fool.
In the dining room, we see
her dancing on a red-bud rose
stuck with thorns she got at school.

She opens up the door at school
to history and tragedy
until the red-bud of the rose
shocks her body; still it goes
and not a thing is left to see
except the shadow of the fool.

Undance the rose in foolish school.
Unplay the fool in tragedy.
Unseen she knows she goes in shadows.

Sapphic Palette

Pale waning moon, still almost full,
white lace dissolving in the spacious blue,
is there, then gone, in fog I'm driving through,
through rolling mist, the day invisible.
The other mountainside returns to light.
I reach the farmer's market with its fruits,
late summer flowers picked and cut from roots,
bouquets in jars, a riot in my sight
at Judy's stand. I have to stop and chat
for purples, petals, pinks. We laugh a lot.
She bags the green and yellow squash I bought
(cut flowers quite beyond my means), and that
is when I glimpse between her buttons, fresh,
white as the moon, her breast's sweet flesh.

GHETTO ON THE FRAUGHT SEA

The Golden Box

I found a golden box on no one's land
and put it in my pocket, mine to keep.
My box is small enough to hide in hand
and bright enough for company in sleep.
My box belongs to childhood and to age.
Inside, the fairies play, the witches fly,
the watchers wake, the readers turn the page
and reach the happy end that makes them cry.
The bible calls us dust, and science stars,
but when you touch my face and kiss my lips,
I see the golden box in all we are,
wearing our golden rings, the rings of ships
sailing and sailing swiftly over seas
full of the fierce sharp wind and sweetest breeze.

Dance of the Violent Calendar

Days and years destroyed, and I plaster pages,
crazy-glue them, hoping to keep protected,
body covered, only my face uncovered,
dancing down Wall Street.

Eighth of June, I dance through the Holland Tunnel,
air-starved, food-starved, love-starved, exhausted, numbly
reach the end. A video shooter asks me
Why did you choose this?

Shoots at me a look full of horror, startled.
How I look reflects in his face. I see it.
Death, no doubt, so ugly, is in me, waits to
rip off my pages,

tell me time is over, turn off my clock and
tear my sheets in half. So I make the pages'
blank verso my paper and write these lines to
keep me a dancer.

Attack of the Fanatics

Breathe, darling, breathe. I cannot
for the life of me patch the ocean.
Ghetto on the fraught sea, blinding.
Did they question the men also?
Or did they only question the women?
The lesbians are policing the lesbians.
Who are you? How do you define yourself?
I list weakly as the interrogators
peer through my telescope backwards.
I am all adrift in the spring fog, trembling.
Port to starboard, keel to mast, mainstay,
my sails a-shiver in the salt-stained waves,
I am unknown to myself, with only a word
my sisters found on Lésvos and gave me.

States

New Jersey

I breathe my first New Jersey air at birth,
a tincture of Passaic. Cut from mother
and on my own, I bike a piece of earth
and settle by the Delaware, another
river, the Crossing re-enacted every
Christmas. The Revolutionary War
fights on below my window, a heavy
vision of booze and black. What I was for
was never clear. I learn my penmanship
and yellow buses, singing, Dick and Jane.
I go to New York City on a trip,
but who I am I cannot ascertain.
The states rave on united in desire
to raise the monster-child a little higher.

Maine

To raise the monster-child a little higher,
observe the lobster traps and smell the sea.
The flimsy sails atop my skiff require
command and there I tack it, hard-a-lee.
I call this good and lucky in a tent,
walking the mossy cliffs, and dipping in
the crashing waves for teenage discontent.
Ever a boy in a batik bikini, skin
golden and glowing, hair light-brown and long,
I spy a hapless sailor on the rocks
caught in a tide and battered by the strong
and endless thrusting ocean. Karma knocks,
and then I learn the low of helplessness,
or try it on again, this tangled dress.

Pennsylvania

Or try it on again, this tangled dress
discarded pool-side at the country home
of Julia Child. I skinny-dip in stress,
in streams, in drunken parties, drag my comb
against my knots and bungles, always hot.
Cloudy and quick the dream of you goes deep
along the deer-trails of my fields, and shot
with shafts, I trip and trust, reveal and leap.
Will music ever sound as sweet again
as on the lost, sad, lonely night I find
you playing cello? Give the lasting pain
a go-away concerto, Scotty, bind
the wounds with music. Then a sound
stirred with her hands turns me around.

Vermont

Stirred with her hands turns me around,
the owl's colossal wings brush by in woods
deep with the leaves that fell in fall to ground
already frozen. Drive my tattered goods
to college, why I couldn't say, a place
at least to last a while, the mountains green,
the apples green, and heaven's open space
shines on the walks I take at night, unseen.
I have to save myself but don't know how.
I have to save myself and read this book.
My chair turns like a clock that won't allow
another sorrow day to slip the hook.
I stop above the pulsing waterfall
listening to pool and splash, my secret call.

New York

Listening to pool and splash, my secret call,
my cell, there's no escaping from the beast
of horns, the force exerted by the wall
keeping me bound inside. To be released
to winter by the Brooklyn Bridge? Or be
the one I recognize and care for, sleep
alone with, give my flowers to. Let me
believe my sewing holds the stitch to keep
the fabric mended. Even though it's tough,
I do the walk and somehow stay alive,
with starving neediness, a shell too rough
to touch. How sad the streets I have to drive,
how inconsolable my steps alone,
I alone could know, and I be shown.

Massachusetts

I alone could know, and I be shown,
the times I could have died but didn't die.
A mountain, tiny rooms, my life my own,
a milk-cow down the road, another try.
The road curves steeply by a frozen creek
higher and higher. Crazed and broken-down,
I walk the woods in spring, my spirit weak.
I lean against an oak tree's giant brown
body, and let the sap that I imagine rise
inside me. Yellow feathers in a pile,
no bird is singing here, and no bird flies.
I drink the milk, deliciously worthwhile,
listen and dream, remember beauty, pain,
the poems I write quietly, the rain.

Missouri

The poems I write quietly, the rain,
the lifetime rushing by without you near,
the window to the lake, the windowpane.
I turn in place and wish I could appear
where people gather comfortably and talk,
but touch like this encouraging more touch
is blossoming on someone else's walk
not mine. You tell me not to mind too much,
remind me many times how troublesome
it could be, how living is the dearest state,
and I believe you, thankful for my crumb.
I fashion this from nothingness, create
myself in this, and when I give this worth,
I breathe my first New Jersey air at birth.

Map

I am alone in the forest by the lake
You know the cove

You will see the red bite on my inner ankle
It will make you melt into me

We are made of exploded stars
My pointed limbs tremble silver for you

I am surrounded by a city of corruption
I die slowly for the solace of your touch

You may travel here by jet and car
And never reach me I am in so deep

The gates stay locked
Nothing normal has ever happened to me

The Natural World

Body   ocean   body of blossoms   touch me
Sea of certainty   am I dreaming now   or
Lilac drowning   throw me a lifeline sometime
      Save me   undress me

Then affection   then in the night   the deeper
After-rain   when grasses and leaves are singing
Notes of such sweet scent that we hurry   gladly
      Into the hidden

Now the stars   the sky   distant planets   pull me
Now the forest whistles   hello!   water!
Body blossom blooming   alone   alone   so
      Touch me   and touch me

I would stand here forever for you

Sawing craving a sympathetic listener
Here I am with a cricket I can marry
Bed-bound losing my day my night my silent
Life my time to make noise losing I write you
Quiet drifting of leaves in fall my only
Cricket   choir of comfort   single sentry

Stripes of light on the ceiling   fields of color
Watch it   watch in the morning witches making
Noon then mixing a potion in the kitchen
Damp and potless   their fingers fling the magic
Balls of waxing and waning hourglasses
Skyward then in a wink the dark begins to
Weaken day   I can see her best in bleakness
Lustrous magnet for monstrous wrongs against her
Always female and wounded   begging entrance
Turned away   she is homeless   raped of all her
Early beauty and gifts my sister Sally

Touch is lake in the evening herons skimming
Homeward (could I be with you tender-voiced one)
Give is forest and trees that line my boulders
(Bring me with you my body's petals scented)
Take is moon of the rain (we listen closely)
Trees again in the morning mossy branches
Wet and weepy (another night of longing
Rooted I and above me leafy motion)
Midnight memo consoles the dreaming sleepers
(How much longer enchantress must I stay here)

Could I bring you a happiness of water
Love like water or air the sound of oceans
Breathing whales and the seabirds flying calmly

Take me closer to you when you're not with me
There are years I remember living solo
Years and years I regret I lost my feeling
Close my eyes my forgetful life and lose me
Waves we are like the ocean waves of water

Give me love of the open window breathing
Say again how the open mouth of breathing
Brings the music and dancing home completely
Dwelling   not an indifferent structure standing
Lives and breathes like a body   trees surround me
Telling stories about the moonlight sliding
On their branches and thighs like hands so softly
Touching feeling and reaching   all night longing
Open open the door and let me love you

Borderline

I enter in to you like a rodeo cowgirl
Who bucks but never falls
Where they ride motorcycles without helmets
The whole sky layered with blue-white-gray colors

If I could only expand past the cover
There to find happiness even without a mother
Entering in to you like the visitation of a butterfly
Delicate motion of wings with unusual patterns

Though I have seen the dead rat carcass
Though unspeakable, nevertheless on the other side
Surely there is the other side
A tenderness of touch and vision

Swimming in some caribbean sea
Facing the barracuda poised just under the surface
Snorkeling, I reach for your hand in a panic
You push me away because trouble is each to one's own

Here in this moment today the crows call
You enter my thoughts from all sides
Like the constant subtle layering of air
Breeze storm calm steady sailing

Yesterday your vision penetrated the walls
It wasn't an emergency, there were no vehicles
The woman in the small red car wasn't driven over a cliff
And the lake below didn't receive her

It wasn't like that at all
Divers, sheriffs, firemen played no part
Farmers slept at last for a few hours
Clerks listened only to silence in their rooms

The homeless, the stricken, the dying find this moment
This moment suffering stops and pleasure begins
The forests give, the oceans take
Your sky and my sky reach the borderline between us

[I cried a river then crossed the river]

I cried a river then crossed the river
I did this on my own without a boat or magic
It was a shallow river, but wide and swift
I carried a bundle of clothes and books

Then my bundle was lost in a flood
I cried so much, I cried an ocean
Then I set sail in an old boat
It was made of driftwood and rags

I crossed the ocean and lost the boat
One big wave tossed me on an island
In this quiet place, my crying dried
I befriended birds and a small cat

I befriended farmers with tiny farms
Who feed me with onions and potatoes
Blackberries, blueberries, cabbages, squash
All year, they keep me well-fed and full

I live in a treehouse in the forest
My tears live in a lake I never touch
Floods are only rain, and storms end
I wait for the sound of waves on the shore

WADING DEEPER IN GREEN WAVES

The Earth

I grabbed my witch's broom too late to sweep the earth
under the rug. The watchers came to creep the earth.

How could I hide my eyes, and which way turn my feet,
without them watching, hand in grave, to reap the earth?

I put my spell on frothing crowds to pacify
the very rocking waves that ride and leap the earth.

In open sky, I leave the clouds, the jets, the stars,
the everlasting icy wind and weep the earth.

To battlements, I cry. Or just begin to cry.
Where is my girl's green jacket? She will keep the earth.

Return my trees. Bring back the rocks and rooks, my treasures
and all streams, swift or slow, the fields, the sheep, the earth.

When my true army carries wounded home, I'll soothe
and heal the crippled seas, the silver deep, the earth.

The Sad Palace of Ill Effects

"Untangle me and weave me into Rug
and place me on the kingdom's palace floor
where every foot can step, and homeless bug
can hide. And store the vacuum by the door."

So ordered by the Queen of Childhood's House
whose spirit had been stolen by a witch.
The queen had snipped the pecker off her spouse,
the king, and he'd become her lonely bitch,
pretty of face and soft to touch, but sad,
so sad he tossed their daughters in a dump.

Now nothing could be done for mum and dad,
the royal Hairbrush stuck with straw, a clump
of youthful wishes lost in faulty lust,
the palace and its owners gone to dust.

Godless

Naked, you disobey and eat the fruit.
The tree was lovely in the spring, but hate,
fat snake of hate, sank fangs in that tree's root,
a sick green venom sealing human fate.
You think it tastes delicious, procreate
and spit. White lightning buzzing in your head,
thundering angels show you to the gate.
In chilly fall you shiver, miss your bed,
wonder about the myths the serpent said,
feel split in two. There's two of you: the bad,
the good, inside one body being fed
the knowledge new to you. You're going mad
and will forever taste the fruit of lies
and be forever charmed by the unwise.

Liebegott

The hell it is, a hell I said,
a monster swamped in plastic bags,
and on the shore, the waves of dead.

Look hot on me and turn me red.
Untie my clothes, or rather rags,
the hell it is, a hell I said.

Oh god of ocean, god of bed,
strike it down and fold the flags,
and on the shore, the waves of dead,

wash them to sleep and bring instead
her puckered lips, not devils' crags,
the hell it is, a hell I said.

A knot pulls harder on a thread,
a taut-held line, and still it sags,
and on the shore, the waves of dead.

Remove the nightmares and the dread,
I'll fuck my love till loving gags
the hell it is, a hell I said,
and on the shore, the waves of dead.

Pepper Mill

She's a grinder, a hill of black pepper,
a deadly spice, no shrubbery in sight.

So my father and mother after the flood
climbed to bed to try for me once more.

We can't think about the morning screwing,
the noon screwing, the evening screwing,

then the piggy baby pooping and peeing,
or the mountain of ground black pepper

on my mother's mashed potatoes
and my father's bacon sandwiches.

Then years of screwing the children,
not screwing like sex, but screwing out of,

not unscrewing the turn of the screw,
but the deeper screwing of the lid on the jar,

shouted damns in the hallway, *damn it,*
screwing out of the ordinary nursery,

the grinding of toys and dolls into rubble.
Look, you, at the sequence of lessons,

corrupted flesh and spirit, how screwing
is grinding, how little the children knew.

Mother Farewell

Mother of arms that never reached for me,
farewell in winter, spring, in summer, fall,
farewell old house, farewell to lawn and hall,
farewell to fields and sky, farewell big tree
that mothered me with leaves entirely.
There was a woman in the house I call
farewell to childhood, building wall on wall
inside herself to break the violent sea,
who saved lost turtles on the winding road,
who stopped the car mid-lane and ran to them
and lifted them, and brought them to the field
or forest they were headed for, each gem
another feather in her mother lode,
each turtle shell, for her, another shield.

Psalm of the Sweetest Water

> *I know the world as it really is.*
> *Endless war, my heart in flames.*
> *But I can smell the sweetest water*
> *When I swim in that water*
> *I am an Angel.*
> —Dorothy Porter, "As it really is"

Inside a man, a fragile crane
in flight sometimes, and often lost,
erects the towers, bombs the towers.
I haven't seen a man inside
the holy temples on his mountains,
terrain a man could claim as his.
A man inside is wilderness
or architecture with a pool
and fountain with a splashing fizz.
I know the world as it really is.

I left the world to look inside,
now an old girl with old girl pains,
ruby treasures stored in chests
engraved with portraits of the queen.
Under my hat, I keep my years
green with grief, unsettled claims,
a skeleton still sharp and bright,
breath, blood, and dust in libraries.
The world I knew with all its games.
Endless war, my heart in flames.

Inside the child I never was,
dropped from above, raised from below,
a baby, pink and splashed with mud,
an ocean braced inside my mind
with difficult books, illegible papers.
I never was, in truth, a daughter,

only a question that couldn't be asked,
only a problem that couldn't be solved,
wearing no one's imprimatur.
But I can smell the sweetest water

and bring my lovers cherry blossoms
picked from centuries of springs.
My anatomy is womanly
with a boy inside in pantaloons
waltzing along like a planet's moons,
cosmic, unearthly, large, and hotter
than tropic noons. I left the world
I used to know, and made a vow
from scratch to hold my silky matter.
When I swim in that water
I am an Angel.

Culture en Femme

You think you're alone but you are not alone.
A black wolf wraps her fur-thick canine around you
while you sleep in *The Sleeping Gypsy* of Rousseau.
She is like a lioness but black and immortal.
Then you have another thought.
Your cat's green eyes. The green
millions of new leaves. You sneeze.
The spirit-wrap squeezes tighter and you curl closer.
You think you're alone with only air in your nose
and bend dancing from the waist like a whistle.
One heron.
You can only report the whistling of creatures
though your body wraps around
a framed view of high-fluff Icarus
and Spenser's lowly pilgrim.
You think you're in a trance only a kiss can break.

In the Healing

Will there be suffering in the healing
Will there be hunger and no food

In the most impossible survival
Will there be thirst and no water

Though I am going to you in torn clothes
You emerge from pure Pacific waves

Though I have fallen below the poverty line
From the day I was born, a steady sickening

Venus, goddess, I believe in you
Burning privately in lost fields of my mind

Faltering and suffering milkweed
Handfuls of wreckage, skeleton, shell

Deus ex Machina

I
Find me, breeze, and blow this memory away:
the sickening kitchens where I couldn't eat,
cockroach in the orange juice, sweet sticky horror,
gagging on a tuna sandwich, I gave up,
sank deeper in the city's muck
until I was cadaver close, dizzy and high
from hunger, a walking spirit, doomed.
How could I giggle, then, about my thinness?
How could my millionaire friends, two artists,
watch me die, poor and starving?
Wasn't I an artist? Hadn't teachers praised me?
They were blind to the arrows stuck in my chest,
my back, my thigh, from all sides shot,
one step from death, one breath from rot.

II
To those who want to meet me face to face,
those gods and goddesses who live above,
so far above they can't imagine want
or have forgotten it, the hungry panic,
the naked wooden chair, the being grateful
forever: thank you, famous poets, critics,
writers, and friends, but I intend to fly—
not in a plane—with wings I grow at home,
great feathered wings of gods and goddesses,
flapping through every shade of paradise.
How else to shake the dirt of hell from off
my shoes? I have to do it here, alone,
I guess, to not be rude, not drag my guts
across the smooth white marble of your floors.

III
Dock-makers navigate the dock. The cove
explodes with moving dock. They walk on it
the way I walk away back to the stove.
Pictures of pleasure rides and boats that sit
and sway in waves all day now summon me
from stove-side to the view of cove and dock
to feel the tides and waves, to stop and see
dock-makers walk on water's city block.
This is my sink, and here I rinse the silver.
This is my kitchen where I cook the food.
I slice the apples, pour the milk and water,
carry the dishes back and forth, and brood
about the dock that I would make for you,
the cove exploding in wild nights for two,
the sweetness of my life in solitude.

Odd Girls

Faith

Oh my darling girl
When did you learn how alone you were?
Days and nights of radiating fiery iron bands of pain
Sleeplessness in some filthy bed where was this
It might have been next to a river or in a borough

Did longing for anything keep you awake?
Working days of danger hunger nights of danger hunger
When blindness broke once there were inklings of this
All my things suffering with a lessening intensity

Did you cling to people in books as if they belonged to you?
First my yearbooks burnt until there was no accounting
My last I was burnt to ash by a policeman in the wasteland

Grace

She opens her portfolio
I stir her buckets of paint and praise her
Stand with her at the dealer in Manhattan

He is silent and I
Bear sorrow with her
While her work is murdered again

Fury walks through the art district
Though she acts like she doesn't care
What does she lack in Manhattan?

Her hand her eye her touch her
Stretched canvas her handmade paper
O the beauty of her colors and lines

Hope

I am a woman writing love letters
That she will never read
Long fields in seasons not yet ripe, wheat uncut
The word not even invented

Because she was gone before I could find her
Her dress only a piece of silk in the river
On her bay horse galloping away
All that shone turning away

The sea wind strong, twisted dandelions
I am a woman writing love letters
To the seagulls and the grass-covered cliff

Verity

I am the unlocked door to the cellar
The cement floor and the flooded washer
The man who said I see everything
The mollusk in the seagull's beak

The lost mutt in a ghetto
The wild unweeded garden bed
The beach towel spread on hot sand
The long fresh nightgown slipping on

The forest and the fiddlehead fern
Orlando and *Paradise Lost*
And though you may not see me
I will always wonder who you are

Patience

I gave you the color green
And did not ask for it back
I gave you the privacy of a shower
I gave you plenty of cherry tomatoes

In a house made of wood from the wildest forests
You ate them three times a day but you did not sing to me
I waited for you every night
While the heavens moaned overhead

How could I give you my happiness if you never noticed me?
I waited long hours at tables and in cars on the highways
I decided to give you more colors
You zipped past me on your way to other colors

Joy

I went past the breakers
With my innocent wishes
I crossed the country on foot
I wanted to feel the Pacific

Wading deeper in green waves
You were there waiting
With your love your sweet sad love
As if only love lives in the world

As if we had never been broken
As if we were never apart
I crossed the country on foot
I went past the breakers

A MOVING JEWEL AT DUSK

Dusk

The water is a moving jewel at dusk
becoming black, with pointed crowns of white.
The day is stealing into pirate night,
the poachers truck away the ivory tusk.
I'll run and dive into the shadow light
to swim the coolly emerald silky lake
or else to drown, to do what it will take
to reach you in the silver sea tonight.
Speak to me now, my awful witch, my gem.
This evening's weight of beauty drags me under
to silence, seaweed, chests of sunken plunder.
A million pearls. Tongue them to me, make them
become your voice, your lips, your breath, your eyes,
the treasure of your arms, your hands, your thighs.

It Gets Very Dark until the Moon Rises

Night falls and darkness drives her pick-up truck
down Highway 86, speeds past the pub
into the hills and hollers, forest, shrub,
and vine, gets tangled, caught, and deeply stuck
until she sinks for good in leaves and muck.
She flicks her cigarette, the sunset stub,
as gunshots hit the town's Masonic club.
In total darkness, she is out of luck

except for this night's moon, which shows her face
slowly at first, first hidden in the air,
but rising, shining, growing, giving dark
a dream, a fantasy of light, a place
less troubled by the lack of day, a fair
of light, with tended paths, a lover's park.

No More

I do not miss you, Susie - no - I do
not miss you. All is gone - I only sit
and stare at nothing from my window - you
are gone - I know - yet I don't feel a bit -
no more than stone can feel the cold - or block
can hear its silence - that it once was warm
and green and birds danced in its branches - rock
is hard to move - cut wood takes any form.

Because sun shines, and sleep has done with me,
I rise, and brush my hair, and dress me - then
I wonder what I am, and how to be,
and who has made me so. It's time again
to wash the dishes - then it's afternoons -
then evenings come, with waxing, waning moons.

Across the Lake

The day sinks quietly across the lake
except for cattle calls across the lake.

Silent the sun's last dip in fairy pink
except some far-off cars across the lake.

A bird in conflict cries itself to sleep,
a dog, a heron, bark across the lake.

Then leaves the light a little at a time,
a rustling hush of leaves across the lake.

All foreign, someone else's comfort lies
in houses made of lies across the lake.

While on her island, Mary pats her cat,
keeping her safe from harm across the lake.

Return Address

> *The poem rushes forth*
> *and would not exist, like so many others,*
> *without a hell for its return address.*
> —Katie Bickham "Supply"

The voices from the lake like messages
reminding me this isn't home, their accents
thankfully dulled by early spring's wild winds,
their laughs, their whistling, dulled by sloshing waves
against their fishing boat, and dulled by clouds
full, fat, and gray, a womb-like sky of north
and south, a civil war of hail, the nests
of newly hatched, the flocks, the squeaking din,
the rosy tree-buds, branches giving birth,
then from my pen, the poem rushes forth.

They leave, a Sunday silence stays, of calls
far as a poor dog's whine, all cushioned in
the sway of limbs of trees and boughs of firs
rehearsing wind until the curtain call
of evening, a silence incomplete on earth
for anyone who listens for another's
story, a scent you track for decades, never
knowing for sure and sighing like a heron.
Here in the air, the lives have many mothers,
and would not exist, like so many others,

without the wind again, exposing blue
and blue exposing sunlight, breaking open
Monday and roars of forests, rusted leaves
soon to be blasted off at last, to start
again, as if they never died last fall.
Spring wind has always been my happiness,
the voice I learned to hear when other voices
shouted. She's lifting my hair like lovers do,
taking me windward with her tree of yes,
without a hell for its return address.

Airstrikes in April

Wind off the lake is winding through the trees,
lifting the wings of bird and butterfly,
tickling the tiny flowers, and my knees,
this season's first bare skin outside, and I,
rich with the pollen, thick and silent, sigh
with every cedar bough and wispy cloud,
the forest on the ground, the distant sky.

The forest wind blows very loud, so loud,
so strong, it shakes the lake and sky, a sound
that muffles other sounds and makes them seem
like muted cries. It roars and lays a shroud
on daily living, makes it like a dream,
and turns it to a war inside the mind,
unsafe and insecure, no treaty signed.

Ars Poetica

She took me home—or what I thought was home,
but was in fact a hell she made for us.
We left *The Sound of Music* with the fuss
that I was making, working out my poem

in sobs. She asked me what was wrong. I said,
"I want to be there," in the Alps, singing,
twirling with her in sunshine. I was clinging
to song, with nothing real to hold instead.

She gave me pain—no comforting the way
most mothers do, I guess. And so I wept
like no tomorrow, out of love. We left
for rainy sidewalks to the car, the day

falling in dusk, the pity I had to make,
the bleak, deserted street I had to take.

Mother Nature

In the ice chest of her air
I write a letter to my other home,
my breath cloud.

Sun tips the very tops of trees,
roots reaching for sky
waving in the icy-fingered wind.

Below, the day is leaving,
and birds that seem only black hurry
somewhere warmer perhaps,

flecks of rushing, and the lake
as a rippling body of silver shades
travels without freezing in its direction

to the cove, the creek, the pasture,
the forest, or the rest of the earth.

GRIPPING HER FALCON

In the Sierra Nevadas

On Glacier Point, my muse appears in tight
blue jeans, a crimson parka, purple vest.
She leans on granite cliffs that pierce the bright
heavens, and smiles above her downy breast.

Clear in the distance not a cloud, just scenes
of sapphire, vistas huge in blocks of rock
and massive slabs in mottled grays. Her jeans
attract my lonely eye. And then in shock,
I see beneath her clothes her naked pose.

O muse seducing me unknowingly—
or do you know? O sunlit skyline rose!
O hummingbird! Your girlie-model knee
angles an upward path along your thigh
where fantasies of lingering glide by.

Herself

The only place to go: inside herself.
Oh, but she didn't want to hide herself.

Outside, the freezing lake, an eagle screaming,
a deathly dampness, crows, the tide, herself.

Cracking the still, some chimes re-bang, re-bong.
When wind caresses her, nerves ride her self.

A breath of icy air inhaled and felt.
A gunshot. Breath exhaled. What died? Her self.

Bleak and abroad, these sounds, sensations, sights.
With her hot thoughts, our girl supplied herself.

She married daylight down her single spine
in wilderness, and dignified herself.

Spring in the Mountains

The rippling surface of the lake
Draws me under to the earth's green eye
Tiny tides beneath the sky
Gold oak leaves cluster, cling, and shake
Old winter's breath, sighing spring
I couldn't say goodbye

Snowflakes in flurries sting

Snow on the ground, owl-cry in the air
Awake in moonlight, richly lit moon blue
Landscape beyond my curtain, past my chair
The calling tremble of the dark's who-whoo
Tender insistent sound sweet to my ear
No other sound slips through the silence here

This chilly room I've grown accustomed to

This spring begins and ends with you
A photograph at midnight pierces through
The window open to the night's new breeze
Like snow but spring entrances through the trees
You're close to me in bed, you speak with ease
Let me not wake to lose this rendezvous

Dream hard of you, the softness of my bed

Ram on by, tornado, and take your thunder
Lightning every second and muddy gushes
Hailstones hit, ants race on the counter
Bees on the ceiling
Outskirts fail again, forget it
Piss them off, ignore them, go on

Air from the open window

Fairy herons on the lake, excited
Vultures in the deadest branches
Crows undoing danger
Spring in the mountains
Mists of pink
Jade raining tassels dangle

Crows

Far in this quiet country, crows. Their calls
make sun-sounds of alarm in distant trees.
They sleep in winter forests, leafless halls
of branches, shaking shadows in a breeze.
They call; they call; I wonder what they say
and who else knows their language. Other birds?
Are crows upset for life, or do they play?
The crows make pictures of the ancient words.
The crows make highways down to hell and back.
The crows make squares and circles on the lake.
The crows, as all girls know, make shimmer-black
in rainbow streaks, and eye you like a snake.
The crows are girls that no one listened to,
whose rituals and wishes no one knew.

The Sky

Take me to heaven, take me folded to the sky.
Open the gate. I must escape and view the sky.

Washed clean by thunderstorms, a gentle lullaby
of midnight air breathes into me, into the sky.

If I could take you with me, sister, wouldn't I?
My whole life has been begging to unscrew the sky.

At noon, the owls and bees from threatened meadows fly,
gathering in the wide blue avenue, the sky.

What other graves will take the lonely left to die?
What is the taste of heaven, honeydew, the sky?

There isn't anyone to ask, the questions sigh.
We swallow dirt, and still we misconstrue the sky.

The Mockers

What rich glass bottle held the picture of
our music teacher, name I can't recall.
I only know I had a twisted love
for her, that she was strange, alone, and tall.
We took the bottle to the field out back,
my childhood friend and I, and dug a grave.
Whatever crazy words we said, I lack
them now. Or did we sing or laugh, I crave
this memory, our kneeling on the ground
one afternoon to place Miss X in earth.
I strain my mind with hope to hear a sound,
even a bird, or leaves in wind, what birth
of folly or regret was brewing then,
what digging up could bring her back again.

Sapphics

Now the clouds release, and the flowing gutters
drown the noise of men in their boats, their chatter.
Stay, sweet rain, and be the fresh sounds I'd rather
beat on my eardrums.

Just a shower. Now tiny birds on branches,
yellow-jewel, cardinal-god, and blue-dart,
clear the air with melodies, sharp, intense, then
suddenly silent.

Saws and trucks annoy from across the water.
How can single woodpeckers, cries of herons,
shrieking crows compete? From the shrinking forest
comes a sad cooing.

Notes on a Lost Quote

> *Now, again, poetry,*
> *violent, arcane, common,*
> *hewn of the commonest living substance*
> *into archway, portal, frame*
> *I grasp for you*
>
> (Adrienne Rich)

I spend the morning searching for the quote about
    nature and poems and feelings
that I must have read not dreamed. It's impossible
to find. There's nothing else to do but write it out.

Sidetracked searching poems in a journal online,
    her life's ease and torment
written right there on her face, one who writes about
a psychiatric ward as if she knew the place.

She must have escaped because she's won prizes,
    her poem close to my heart lately,
gentle, sharp, sad, compassionate. I copy and paste it
in my thoughtful notes of effort and disappointment,

retract my jealous petty fault-finding, I love her poem,
    really. Quote still missing.
No more can I be severed from your side
Than can yourself yourself in twain divide.

(Shakespeare) I go through a series of blue doorways
    twisting my skeleton key sideways,
prizeless, wardless, in freshening wind off the lake,
away from words and screen, with my young leaves.

Gender

I'll make a mystery of your history,
sayeth the Lord, resisting my attempt
to grasp the fundamentals, learn the bee
and bird, decipher what the pharaoh dreamt.

The jester jumps to England and the Queen,
the stage, the castle, and the hangman's noose.
Behave or be beheaded sets the scene
in which the witches' hats and shoes fly loose.

You will remember me, the queer-voiced Mary,
gripping her falcon. Let me live. And let
us marry on the ship's bright deck of cherry
where we will settle our sad century's debt.

I built a room to write my truthful tome,
and here it is at last, my love, my home.

Notes

"In the Healing." The line "Will there be suffering in the healing" is from Muriel Rukeyser's poem "Body of Waking."

"No More." Based on an August, 1854, letter from Emily Dickinson to Susan Gilbert.

"The Earth." The line "How could I hide my eyes" is from Hilda Doolittle's "Helen in Egypt."

"Sentimentality." Title inspired by this quote from Patrick Donnelly on *Poetry Daily:* "If a love poem is going to go off the rails, it's usually in the direction of sentimentality. Some very good poems generate excitement from how much sentimentality they risk..."

"It Gets Better." Title derived from this project: "In September 2010, syndicated columnist and author Dan Savage created a YouTube video with his partner Terry Miller to inspire hope for young people facing harassment. In response to a number of students taking their own lives after being bullied in school, they wanted to create a personal way for supporters everywhere to tell LGBT youth that, yes, it does indeed get better." (itgetsbetter.org)

Acknowledgments

Many thanks to the editors of the following publications, in which these poems appeared, sometimes in earlier versions:

Adrienne: "States"
American Arts Quarterly: "It Gets Very Dark until the Moon Rises"
Angle: "Sapphic Palette," "Dusk"
Autumn Sky Poetry: "The Mockers," [I am the unlocked door to the cellar]
Califragile: "Attack of the Fanatics"
Cimarron Review: "Crows," "In the Healing," "The Natural World"
Citron Review: "It Gets Better" (runner-up in Queer contest)
Crab Orchard Review: [What could October ever satisfy]
IthacaLit: "A Political Poem with Emotional Parts"
OCHO: "Liebegott"
Prelude: "The Sad Palace of Ill Effects," "Map"
Rattle: "Alone in Love," "Ars Poetica"
San Diego Reader: "In the Sierra Nevadas" (winner sonnet contest)
SWWIM: "The Earth" (nominated for Pushcart Prize), "Pepper Mill"
Taos Journal of International Poetry & Art: "Mother Nature"
The Awl: [I cried a river then crossed the river]
The Gay & Lesbian Review: "Attack of the Fanatics," "Life Study," "The Mockers," [When is the last ferry leaving for the island]
What Rough Beast: "Airstrikes in April"
Women's Review of Books: "Gender," "From the Notebooks of Margaret Mead"

Anthologies
Deranged (Picaroon Poetry): "It Gets Better"
Nasty Women Poets (Lost Horse Press): "Liebegott"

Headmistress Press Books

Nuts in Nutland - Mary Meriam, Hannah Barrett
Lovely - Lesléa Newman
Teeth & Teeth - Robin Reagler
How Distant the City - Freesia McKee
Shopgirls - Marissa Higgins
Riddle - Diane Fortney
When She Woke She Was an Open Field - Hilary Brown
God With Us - Amy Lauren
A Crown of Violets - Renée Vivien tr. Samantha Pious
Fireworks in the Graveyard - Joy Ladin
Social Dance - Carolyn Boll
The Force of Gratitude - Janice Gould
Spine - Sarah Caulfield
Diatribe from the Library - Farrell Greenwald Brenner
Blind Girl Grunt - Constance Merritt
Acid and Tender - Jen Rouse
Beautiful Machinery - Wendy DeGroat
Odd Mercy - Gail Thomas
The Great Scissor Hunt - Jessica K. Hylton
A Bracelet of Honeybees - Lynn Strongin
Whirlwind @ Lesbos - Risa Denenberg
The Body's Alphabet - Ann Tweedy
First name Barbie last name Doll - Maureen Bocka
Heaven to Me - Abe Louise Young
Sticky - Carter Steinmann
Tiger Laughs When You Push - Ruth Lehrer
Night Ringing - Laura Foley
Paper Cranes - Dinah Dietrich
On Loving a Saudi Girl - Carina Yun
The Burn Poems - Lynn Strongin
I Carry My Mother - Lesléa Newman
Distant Music - Joan Annsfire
The Awful Suicidal Swans - Flower Conroy
Joy Street - Laura Foley
Chiaroscuro Kisses - G.L. Morrison
The Lillian Trilogy - Mary Meriam
Lady of the Moon - Amy Lowell, Lillian Faderman, Mary Meriam
Irresistible Sonnets - ed. Mary Meriam
Lavender Review - ed. Mary Meriam

VIOLET

SEA

GREEN

DUSK

FALCON

www.ingramcontent.com/pod-product-compliance
Lightning Source LLC
Chambersburg PA
CBHW071234090426
42736CB00014B/3070